CW00972393

GET CONSCIOUS

Wake up to your Personal Power, Magnificence and Divine Connection

By Dr. Risha Joshi

Volume 1, Series 1

Acknowledgements

This book has taken 32 years to come together. Not that I have been writing it for that long but this is the length of time that I have been on the planet! This is the length of time that I have been making and learning from my mistakes, studying and applying principles, watching and understanding the world around me, observing and querying that which has been dictated to me and experiencing life as I know it. Every single experience has landed me where I am now - where I want to be. For this I will always be grateful to *all* that life has offered, including the challenges, difficulties and discomforts.

My Father and my Mother, my Uncle and Aunt - *Bapa and Motima* - who are like my parents - have given me my foundation. Without my upbringing there is no way I would have aligned with my purpose − to help those who suffer from negative emotions, feelings of disempowerment, fear and lack of connection. To you I will always be grateful because you have taught me the value of unconditional love and have supported me in so many ways throughout my life. Thank you for having the courage to push past your anxieties, worries and fears so that I may fulfil my dreams. You gave up yours so that I could have mine. I love you and I am humbled by you. You have shown me the true meaning of strength, resilience and selflessness.

To my brother, *Rishi*, who I love more than life itself. You move me with your strength, love for the world and your balance. Thank you for always being there and helping me like Dad would have if he was here. I would be nothing without you.

To my parents' Guru – *Sri Ram Sharma Acharya* – thank you for showing my parents the way and for teaching them love and resilience through their difficult times. Thank you for being the light when they were in the dark.

To my Aunt, *Muni Masi* and the three jellies, *Pooja*, *Shivani* and *Vibhuti* – thank you for loving me unconditionally. I love you to the moon and back. You make me feel like I have come home.

To my Soul Mates, *Jag, Radhika, Kelly, Chan, Lucy, Karen Sophia, Alexander* and *Kenneth* who have helped me beyond belief. You have made me stronger and given me confidence. You have been there to pick me up when I didn't have the strength to do it myself and you have shown me the way. I am so lucky to have found you, or rather, thank you for finding me! We have some amazing times ahead of us!

To my dogs, *Winston* and *Yogi*, you can't read this but you are adored!

To *Daisy*, you've been there for me through thick and thin. Thank you for always making me smile. I'm lucky to have you as a friend. To *Ravi*, thank you for being an oracle and always imparting your wisdom and logic without judgement. Thank you both for letting me be me and for putting up with my ways.

To *Tanay, Robert and Jags* – thank you for supporting me in all of the 'little' ways which were actually the very big ways. Thank you for listening and being my sound boards. You helped me to expand my mind.

Finally, to anyone else who has loved, supported and encouraged me – I will never forget your kindness. And to anyone who has given me *any* difficult life experience - thank you for the lessons.

Above all, thank you to the Universe, for loving me throughout my life, for guiding me through my troubles and for your connection.

To all of you I dedicate this book – you are the reason why I am, where I am and for that, I will be eternally grateful.

All my love x

Contents

Dedicated to my Father,

Chandresh Joshi

My Inspiration. My Source of Strength.
Always in my Heart.

Introduction:

Dear Reader,

This book has been compiled with the intention to humbly assist anyone who wishes to break free from a cyclical, unfulfilled and uninspiring life. It has been written for anyone who believes that there is more to life than meets the eye. It is for those of you who have not yet found your purpose or your passion and are caught up in the daily 'grind' of life without feeling much satisfaction or joy. It is for anyone who wants more for themselves and for others but do not feel that this is possible or that life is consistently working against them. It is for you if you feel stagnant and limited yet desire to grow. This book is for you if you want to make a change but feel fearful of upsetting the status quo at the risk of balance and stability. It is for anyone who feels at loss in their relationships, finances, health, levels of joy, peace or love. If this sounds like you, if you are seeking more from life - congratulations on taking the first step towards having a beautiful one.

I'm here to tell you that you are far more powerful and in control than you could possibly imagine. I'm here to tell you that there are no mistakes in nature – that includes yourself and your circumstances. I'm here to let you know that you are loved, supported and guided more than you could ever realise. I'm here to let you know that success is a *state of mind* that is reflected in our surroundings. There is a Divine order of which you are a vital component part. How can I say this with such conviction? Because there was a point in my life where I was sceptical, disconnected, depressed and felt downright hopeless. I took charge of my mind and nurtured it. Now it serves *me* - rather than me serving it. As a result, I feel genuine guidance, connection, excitement, fulfilment, peace, joy and love *consistently* and *regularly* - and when ever I don't - I know how to get back to those states quickly. I took charge of my personal suffering and decided to do something about it. The Universe met me at the level that I met myself and I have never looked back. As a result, I feel aligned with my purpose and my passion and couldn't be more at peace. My greatest realisation has been that in order to change my life for the better, the work was never needed outside of myself - it was *always* internal.

No matter where you are in life, it is my intention to help you realise that happiness and sadness are choices that we make on a day to day, minute to minute and second to second basis. The mirroring of our choices can be seen around us, in our experiences and circumstances. If you want to understand what you think about on a consistent basis - just look around you. Through the awareness of unconscious cycles of thinking, it is my intention to help you realise your magnificent creative abilities and your personal power for change.

The journey from sadness to happiness; from emptiness to deep satisfaction; from fear to love; from scarcity to abundance; from despair to hope, always begins in those life changing, split-second, *(often rock bottom)* moments, when we decide 'NO MORE'. Massive change happens during these times where the pain of staying where we are is greater than the fear of change.

When we reach these stages in our lives, *huge* transformation is possible. They are the *markers* of success and growth. By you acquiring this book, you have consciously or unconsciously, made a decision. You have bravely stated your intention for change.

When the mind expands, it can not go back to it's original state. By choosing to read this book, you have opened up an opportunity to expand your mind and your horizons – *regardless* of whether or not the book is actually read. This desire to search is the greatest catalyst for change. I urge you to run with this opportunity, to build momentum and to not look back. It is for this reason, I thank (and encourage *you* to thank) your struggles and dissatisfaction, as without them you would not be on track to seeking the maximum fulfilment of your desires and the deep sense of satisfaction from life that is possible through continued personal expansion.

The principles outlined in this book are drawn from my own personal experience, intuitive guidance and teachings from around the world. I have spent over 20 years studying and applying these principles and I now feel connected enough to my inner being to write this book for you. These teachings have come from some of the happiest and most fulfilled people on the planet and also wisdom stored in my heart – an innate pure wisdom that is accessible to ALL of us. Subsequently, the contents of the book may resonate with you at a soul level. It may just *feel* 'right' and make sense. If it does, I urge you to use it and continue your personal development. It is a firm belief of mine that self investment is the *best* investment that any of us can make and it *always* leads to success.

I have spent time, being driven by my curious mind, selecting the CORE patterns in the behaviour, mind set, teachings and mental make-up of the worlds' most successful and fulfilled people. I have presented the concepts behind their success in neat, bite-size chunks throughout the book. It is important to explain at this point, that by *success* I mean our ability to accomplish *any* desire regardless of what is considered to be 'success' by society's standards. For some, success may mean feeling love, for others, it may mean earning a trillion dollars. No matter what you want to achieve, the concepts in this book may serve your purpose. It is my belief that the ultimate form of success is *freedom*; freedom from anything that prevents you from expanding into your greatest self. True emotional freedom leads to peace, joy, love, fulfilment and growth and these are the undeniable markers of success. With these markers firmly intact *first*, any goal you put your mind to is achievable. The trick is to master the mind, which can learn to fear the '*run up*' to success and throw obstacles in the way. Undetected, the mind even has the ability to hinder it. It is in doing the necessary work at *this* level that we open ourselves up to opportunities, abundance and the fulfilment of our desires – all of which are available and waiting for us in endless supply. This level of freedom is our birth right.

Every single concept in this book can be expanded into theses of their own but for the purposes of this book, I have attempted to make the principles easy to understand and digest, with the scope of further expansion if you wish to continue your personal inquiry. This is something that I would encourage. Just like the exponentially-expanding Universe, expansion is something that we naturally desire. In its own right, it is my aim to encourage broader minded thinking and to open up your eyes to some underlying principles which, when mastered, lead to unshakeable power, deep satisfaction, increased levels of joy and abundance in all forms.

I encourage you to commit to the reading of this book and even refer back to it over time. Its digestible nature allows you to do this with ease and can act as a useful *'pick me up'* during times when you feel the need to reconnect and gain perspective. Read it at a pace that feels comfortable to you and take time to absorb the concepts. This may be tricky at times as some of the ideas may tap into and even *challenge* your current belief systems which you may be relying upon, subconsciously, for emotional stability. Try to become aware of these areas of resistance and consider the prospect that the uncomfortable change is pointing you towards those aspects of yourself that warrant exploration. You may find that some of the belief systems are perfectly valid or you may find that you are unknowingly holding onto a belief that is flawed, irrelevant or outdated. *These* are the beliefs that hold you back. Give yourself time to explore your mind. The awareness of it will assist in the clearing of those mental factors that block your growth. Fundamentally, take what is useful and that which resonates with you, expand on these topics if you wish, add what is uniquely your own and discard the rest. This is true authenticity.

Finally, if this book serves you, pass it on to someone else so that it may serve them too.

In the writing of this book, I am sending you buckets of love and light. I wish you a *truly* beautiful life.

In divine friendship,

Risha

xox

Namasté

My Soul honours your soul.
I honour the place in you where the entire Universe resides.
I honour the light, love, truth, beauty and peace within you,
because it is also within me.
In sharing these things, we are united. We are the same. We
are One.

Chapter 1: Are you sleeping?

"When everyone is thinking alike, then no one is thinking"

— Benjamin Franklin

Our minds are all that we have.

Everything we have done, everything we are currently doing and everything we *will* do, is determined by our minds. The moulding of our personalities, the depth of our interpersonal connections, the quality of our relationships, the minor and major decisions that we make and *how* we perceive the world - ALL depend upon our thoughts. What we think, we become. The quality of our lives is *directly* related to the quality of our thoughts.

Experience gets filtered into our minds via our senses and then interpreted, analysed and assessed. The more emotionally impactful the experience, the greater the likelihood of it becoming ingrained within our minds. Even those experiences with *zero* emotional impact get stored. These 'stored' thoughts, if *called upon* and repeatedly stimulated over time, become our active *beliefs* about the various aspects of life we have exposure to. They become our convictions and our versions of 'truth'. These experiences and their interpretations, become the models for our lives and influence our view of the world as a whole. The way in which we process our experiences i.e. *how* we view our personal stories and the meanings that we attach to them, plays a huge role in our outlook. Depending on the nature of our beliefs, they either help us to grow or they restrict us.

Over time, we have become efficient *accumulators* of experience, thoughts, feelings and beliefs. We use our experiences and our interpretations of them to guide our lives and to form our identities. Although of referential benefit, it may be clear to see that these added 'layers' have the ability to conceal our authentic nature. It may also be clear to see that if we place too much importance on our mental 'accumulations' we risk suppressing our capacity to grow beyond them. We learn how to act, look, think and behave based on what we have adopted from our childhood, our historic experience and our external environments. Our ability to detach from those thoughts that limit us is directly related to our capacity to feel happiness, joy, peace, love and our capacity to grow – growth being the marker of *all* forms of success. When we can observe and sort through the contents of our minds, we can become powerful orchestrators of our lives via the selection of high quality thoughts that encourage our expansion.

When we are unaware of our minds, our interpretations of experience can become our consistent *offerings* that become more and more ingrained within the mind. They are innately limited as they are solely based on past events and historic experience. This gives our regular thoughts the ability to drag us *out* of the present moment hindering our ability to fully experience the unique *now* moments. The mind is the 'springboard' for the creation of our own worlds and although *dipping* into the past and future tenses can be useful for growth, it is of maximum benefit to us when they are used as references to *supplement* present experience - not to replace them. The present moment is where the *greatest* opportunity for growth lies and it is also where historic cycles can be broken in order to allow innovation and creativity. The present moment is where *success* is found.

When it comes to our sense of being or the direction in which we take our lives, whether we feel good or bad, happy or sad, it is all dependent upon our ability to balance this process of selecting high quality thoughts and residing in the present moment. Every discovery, every work of art, every invention, every innovation we see around us has come from a single, creative, present-moment, *high-quality* thought which gained enough momentum to actualise.

'Whether you think you can or whether you think you can't, you are right'

- *Henry Ford*

Our minds are heavily responsible for the differences in our success levels, our varying levels of health and the quality of our relationships. The mind regulates and enhances the stories that we tell ourselves about the meanings of our life experience until our life experiences *become* the meanings that we have assigned. This occurs as the mind attempts to serve its primary objective – *optimisation* and *efficiency*. When we 'ask' it to believe a particular concept by means of our regular thoughts on the topic, the mind will enhance that particular thinking process. Our repeated thoughts turn into what we believe to be *true* about life and the choices we make reflect our beliefs back to us.

Our beliefs can be seen as the *'lens'* through which we project ourselves. These 'lenses' become our paradigm - our way of seeing the world INTO reality. For instance, if you believe that the world is a dark and horrid place to be in, your lens will *hone in* on those aspects of life that validate your argument. If you believe the world is full of opportunity, you will find them everywhere. Our mind is the *sole determinant* of our lives. It would serve us well to get acquainted with it.

Despite its multiple functions, how the mind works is poorly understood. For instance, modern Science hasn't yet been able to shine much light on the *entire* function of the mind and its capabilities. Many of us are not really aware of how our minds work on a *personal* level nor its impact on the quality of our lives. Mental health disorders such as anxiety and depression are on the rise, without very much advancement in the cure other than medication which often act to brush the deeper issues 'under the carpet'. It is my belief that many of these disorders are symptoms of disconnection – disconnection between the body, mind and the spirit. Through unconscious, programmed patterns of thinking, we have forgotten how to integrate ourselves - to be and feel whole and to grow. We have disconnected from our unique, authentic nature which desires expression, resulting in disharmony and *dis-ease*. There are symptoms of this problem on more extreme, obvious scales but we may also be suffering from this disconnection on more subtle levels. On a regular basis, we may be choosing thoughts that limit us, the evidence of which may be observable in our undesirable circumstances and how *well* we feel.

Pain is inevitable but suffering is optional. Much needless suffering exists even amongst those who appear to 'have it all'. It all boils down to one single factor – our ability to choose *high quality* thoughts. When our minds are confined and discouraged from expanding, disharmony exists. This disharmony is always caused by a fear based, limiting thought process. Due to this limitation, we go *against* the flow of life - which is expansive in nature. Authenticity is not readily encouraged by society. We are programmed to think alike, to dress alike, to look a particular way and to conform. Above all, we are trained to fear going *against* these standards. These restrictive patterns of thinking prevent growth, which is then reflected in our well being.

There has never been a greater need to answer the question *"what leads to sustained happiness, well being and fulfillment?"*. Every single one of our endeavors and every single one of our pursuits holds this question at its core. It is the goal of every action. No matter which approach is adopted - we all want to feel good.

Many of us have learnt how to become *reactive* to our external and internal environments. This is a disempowering way to function.

We have used the massive ocean of thoughts that are present within our minds to *dictate* our lives haphazardly, without sifting through and carefully selecting thoughts which are of benefit to our growth. To some degree, we have lost our mental filters and have learned to react to *every* stimulus that life offers, using '*tried and tested*' methods to follow through. It is a form of mental slavery. We have placed limits on our authentic nature by living a hugely mentally regulated life. This goes against our authenticity and innate desire to grow. How many of us unknowingly ride the waves of fear-based thoughts because it is the way we have always operated? Do you worry excessively about the future or the past? Do you worry about fitting in? Do you worry about what other people think of you? Are you aware of what drives you? Is it love or is it fear? How many of us really understand where our thoughts and beliefs have come from? Do they even *belong* to you? Are they even *relevant*? How many of us have looked to *see*?

It is quite clear that of the some 60,000 thoughts and stimuli that we are exposed to each day, not *all* of them will be of benefit to our well being, not all of them will direct our lives in a positive way, not all of them belong to us, not all of them are relevant, not all of them lead to happiness and not all of them are anything other than observations of our external environments. Yet *all* of them make their way into our minds. It is no wonder that in the midst of this *plethora* of thought, without a selection criterion in place, we feel out of control, fearful, confused, unhappy and disempowered. Whilst we feel these emotions - fulfilment, joy, happiness, peace, love and success are not possible.

It is important to give the mind the respect it deserves and to recognise its power. The mind is *extremely* efficient. If we suffer a burn to our hand as a child, for instance, we will not need to learn the lesson again and again by going through the exact same process repeatedly. We will immediately detect the source of danger and takes steps towards removing ourselves from the situation. Uncontrolled and unaware, our minds may even make us fearful of any form of heat! The mind recognises what is required for our personal safety and without direction, can go on 'high alert' for anything that can be potentially dangerous, as well as that which even remotely resembles the perceived threat.

It may also *bypass* multiple mental steps to get to the outcome (*safety*) but when left to its own devices, the mind will often bypass logic and reason. Although efficient at being on the 'look out', the mind has a tendency to lose its ability to discern. For instance, you may even see the word FIRE and the same 'alarm bells' may start ringing in your mind, warning you of danger. In this way, the mind is a master at survival and therefore of great value to us when *real* danger is present. It is not necessarily best suited to understand what real, life threatening danger *is*. The problem is, that the mind learns to see threats to our existence in multiple aspects of our lives that are not necessarily life threatening or harmful but are just based on historic memory. These memories - although predominantly *only* exist within our minds - can cause a huge amount of fear to develop, especially when repeatedly triggered. Often the things we fear are actually the *very* things that help us to expand and achieve our desires. We have learnt to avoid pain 'at all cost', not recognizing that pain is often *essential* for our growth. It is how the greatest lessons can be learnt. In this way the minds ability to discern and its reliability is often questionable.

An example of the minds inability to discern is when we hold unhealthy beliefs about whether or not we *fit in* to society. The mind may encourage us, based on this belief, to look, accumulate or behave in a certain way. This fear of not being accepted, when stimulated over time, has the ability to form an ingrained *conviction* that, unless we conform, we will not be accepted as our authentic selves. This leads to the fear of <u>not being worthy or the threat of not being loved</u> and, therefore, a perceived sense of danger. This perceived threat to *two* of our basic human needs becomes reinforced over time and dictates aspects of our being. We build barriers and alter our authentic selves in order to avoid 'danger' and perceived pain. The opposing, healthier perspective would be the belief that we are all *unique* and a belief that encourages personal expression but the 'unconscious' mind may hone in on the self deprecating thoughts based *purely* on habit. This manner of thinking can become crippling unless we increase our *awareness* and select empowering thoughts to build momentum on. The mind in this sense is a very efficient 'watch dog' which, in itself, has obvious benefits but without 'training', the mind has the ability to become *hyper* alert. It is my belief that this 'hyper alert' state and our ingrained fears are responsible for ALL forms of *dis-ease*.

Our basic needs include the need to feel safe, significant, connected and loved, to have stability and variety - yet all around us are messages that make us feel the contrary. From messages on billboards, to what we see on the news, to the stories we are told throughout our lives - we unconsciously *adopt* these messages and our minds act to serve their existence. The good news is that we all have the innate ability to become more *aware* and to understand our minds. This means that we have <u>*choice*</u>.

We hinder ourselves in the psychological *decision making* processes. We defeat ourselves by living life *unconsciously* and unaware of our minds. We defeat ourselves by not giving our mind the attention it deserves – by not loving it and nurturing it. The first thing we need to do in order to become powerful creators of our lives is to consider the notion that we are *more* than just highly efficient programs and from there we can transition into 'waking up' and becoming more *conscious*.

Chapter 2: The function of the Mind

'If you correct your mind, the rest of your life will fall into place'

- *Lao Tsu*

In the previous chapter we discussed the impact of our thoughts on our personal realities. We discussed how they shape our minds, our beliefs and our circumstances. We also discussed how the quality of our thoughts influence our success levels. Recognising the significance of our thoughts and mastering them can seem a daunting challenge. How do we take charge of our thinking and our realities? How do we *rewire* ourselves for success? The answer lies in understanding how the mind works.

One of the functions of the mind is to translate energy.

Everything in life is energy in motion. All that our senses are able to detect has an energetic configuration or pattern that the mind translates and gives meaning to. For instance, when we eat an apple, what we are actually tasting (at a quantum level) is a specific arrangement of *electric* and *magnetic* energy held together with the help of particles. It is in the arrangement of these energetic bonds that the apple is tasted and identified. The *forces* that connect the particles together is what we taste - not the particles themselves. The mind translates the energy within the food, processes it and absorbs it into its own energy field. The same principle applies to the hearing of sound, the sensation of touch, seeing, smelling and understanding intuitive guidance. The mind detects *vibration* (which ALL particles continuously undergo) and the subsequent *energy* generated by means of the physical senses and creates its own interpretation. This is how *every* aspect of our external environment is perceived and how it makes its way into our mind space.

When we look at a stationary object, we see it as solid and rigid through our senses. On a microscopic level however, the atoms - the building blocks - do not even *touch* each another. They are held together by means of this invisible, electromagnetic force, forming the structure of the perceived object. Furthermore, the atoms that make up the object are approximately *99.9% space*, yet they have the ability to form something that appears to be quite the *opposite* of space. Even our bodies are predominantly empty space yet we see fully functioning, 'solid' structure. It is said that if all of the *actual* substance of our body was condensed - it would be the size of a pinhead! There is virtually **no** substance to anything that we are able to see, feel, touch, smell or hear. All matter is predominantly energy in motion.

Our senses are innately limited. As you are reading this book, for instance, it may be difficult to imagine that you are travelling hundreds of thousands of miles *per second* through space whilst physically feeling 'stillness'. The mind also has the ability to further distort translated energy vibration through *emotional* attachment. For example, if a certain song reminds you of a difficult time in your life, hearing the song - even decades down the line - can cause the resurfacing of emotions linked to those historic, difficult times. This attachment can change the way in which the song is perceived as a whole. Even if the song is composed to meet perfect musical standards, you may feel discomfort and dislike the experience of listening to it due to its emotional significance. In itself, the minds ability to detect energy and translate it does not create variations in perspective but its ability to add *meaning* does. This can lead to the existence of multiple perspectives or versions of 'reality' between individuals. For this reason, reality is sometimes considered an *illusion* due to the limitation of our senses, the fluid nature of energy, the massive variation in mental interpretations and the significant emotional 'distortion' of information that is possible.

Every aspect of life is held in balance through energetic interaction − an *invisible* force. What we see as distinguished separation between form is not separation at all. Even our skin is not solid at a quantum level. Energy courses through every aspect of the Universe connecting it by means of an invisible, energetic 'blueprint' or 'web' *upon* which the varying forms of life are suspended in energetic balance. This electromagnetic background grid is the only 'constant' and is the backbone of all existence. The mind translates a very limited aspect of it and even *that* is subject to interpretation.

There is more to life than meets the eye. Our physical eyes only have the ability to see 1% of the entire electromagnetic spectrum. We can not see the ultraviolet light that a bumble bee can when it hovers from flower to flower. We can not see X-rays, microwaves or even effectively in the dark. We can not hear the high pitched noises that a dog can hear. Elephants can detect the call of another from 3 miles away and are even reported to detect changes in the environment prior to an earthquake. Their versions of reality are *very* different to ours. Nothing that we are able to experience through our 5 senses is as it seems, yet we often believe with *complete conviction* that our individual beliefs, realities and perceptions are the complete representation of what is true and what is not. In this sense, what is 'real' is subject to so much interpretation that it is virtually impossible to define.

'The only true wisdom is in knowing that you know nothing'

- Socrates

Although we can use certain laws and principles that are based on *repeatable* and *predictable* results i.e. the pursuits of Science, to help us to define *how* life 'works' - these processes can be limited due to their foundations being set only on historic experience.

Science can prove certain aspects of life but not the whole picture. The only *undeniable* reality is that of the underlying energetic 'grid' and not the realities created by our minds. This 'grid' or 'field' is a highly coordinated, mathematically precise *blueprint* that lies *beneath* all form – almost like 'glue' holding the entire Universe together. In order to positively influence our lives, it is far more powerful and profound to create influence at the *core* level of existence – at the level of energy. Being equipped with (a) the awareness of our minds (b) the knowledge of how our in-built, powerful *translators* of energy, our minds, operate and (c) the energetic influence we have on the field by means of our thoughts and emotions - it may be clear to see that we have an evolutionary advantage. Understanding the principles of energy and our individual, profound impact on the blueprint prevents the needless suffering caused by the cycles of unsuccessful attempts at changing our versions of reality from the outside, *in*. These cycles can be compared to the attempt at removing the raw ingredients of a cake *after* it has been baked. It is not totally impossible but significantly arduous. By understanding the impact of working at the core level of form, we can create sustained, dependable change in our lives. By working on ourselves, the energy of our thoughts and by understanding how powerful our emotions are, we can learn how to 'manipulate' energy to create positive change in our lives. This manner of bringing about change is deeply fulfilling and empowering.

Not only does the mind translate, it also emits energy into its surroundings via our bodies and through to our external environments. We are *constantly* emitting and radiating energy vibration, the most powerful of which are our emotions which are *fuelled* by our thoughts. Thoughts and emotions create *tangible* changes within the body, from fluctuations in temperature and heart rate to physical changes in the tissues. Emotions that stem from fear cause an overall *contraction* in our energy, which leads to changes such as contraction in our muscles, poor posture and an increase in our heart rate. Feeling love *expands* our energy, causing effects such as the expansion of our chests and the reduction in our heart rate. These internal changes in turn, impact our external environment which, as mentioned previously, are not separate due to energetic fluidity that exists between all things.

A thought is a physical movement within the body that can build enough momentum to create an emotional response. Over time, this can lead to changes in the physical body and our external environments. The best way to influence the *mind* is to acknowledge and use these emotional, physical and external responses to identify the thoughts that are in operation. Similarly, the best way to influence our *external* environments is to create at the level of thought. For this reason, strong connection to our bodies and our emotions leads to the intelligence that is required to identify and direct our thoughts and our lives. The trouble is that often trauma and pain from the past can lead to *disconnection* between our mind, our body and our emotions. This occurs in order to avoid feeling massive pain. We can shut ourselves off from *feeling* all together. This disconnection leads to further suffering and limitation on our expansion and our fulfilment.

Our thoughts create major ripples in the energetic web of life. We have the ability to channel thought towards favourable circumstances. When we understand how the mind works and when we know what we want, we can become *deliberate* creators. By influencing the *energy* of our desires, we are able to impact form at the most fundamental level. Like a snowball, sustaining the momentum of desirable thoughts and emotions will eventually lead to guaranteed action and outcome. *Acting* towards our desires is not the primary step in creation - the thinking and emotional energies need to marry first. Those who merely act without emotional and energetic integrity, often find that they struggle to fulfil their desires and if they do, they struggle to maintain them. The <u>energetic</u> marriage between thought, emotion and action in order to actualise our desires is also known as manifestation. Manifestation can help us or hinder us based on the thoughts we practice most often – negative or positive, energetically contracting or energetically expanding. If this sounds like a difficult process to master – you should know that if you have the ability to think, you have been carrying out this process your entire life! We have been influencing the field *consistently* by our thoughts and emotions - the manifestations of which, by means of quantum law, we see all around us. This is how powerful each one of us is in our creative abilities. To change our circumstances from undesirable to desirable is not that difficult. It involves the *exact* same process but directed in the opposite way! We just need to become more aware of what *exactly* it is that we are manifesting.

The advancement of technology and the overall advancements of mankind have been manifested in the same way - by the channelling of thought towards ideas, dreams and goals until they have materialised. *Everything* we see around us is the manifestation of form via the sustained, channelled energy of thought.

The mind is also a highly efficient and well regulated storage system and has the capacity to store *huge* quantities of information. In fact, it does not forget a thing! As mentioned in the previous chapter, our minds are efficient accumulators of our internal and external, current and historic experiences, our perceptions and our interpretations. We have access to an *endless* supply of 'translated' energy and this gives us a huge number of **options** to select our mental 'direction' from on a day to day, minute to minute, second to second basis. In the absence of a decision making process, however, we can also feel confused and suffer from *information overload*. Unless we recognise the power we have over a mental 'sifting' process, this information overload can lead to fear, stress, anxiety, helplessness, burnout and a whole host of negative emotions. We can feel depression and despair whilst we *wade* through the confusion of the mind, *habitually* selecting the thoughts that are self deprecating or fear based in nature. Empowerment is recognising that you are in control of which thoughts you choose to pay attention to and that you *always* have a choice. Mastering this art leads to a profound level of freedom and the deep understanding that the mind is best suited when it is of service to you - not when it acts as an authority.

When we select a particular thought to pay attention to, whether it be consciously or unconsciously, a domino effect is created. The thought gains energy by finding more thoughts that are similar in nature from the plethora of thoughts that are available in the mind. The initial thought expands and gains momentum – an innate *desire* and characteristic of energy in general. Unless interrupted, this process (in the fertile 'soil' of our minds) is sustained and self perpetuating. One single thought can build enough energy and momentum to not only affect our emotions, our body and our biochemistry but also our circumstances and our lives. The minds ability to store such vast quantities of information can give us choice but can also hinder us unless we *consciously* direct it. Unless we master it.

Not only will sustained thoughts on a particular topic lead to internal and external change, they will also create physical changes in the brain. Consistent thinking patterns lead to altered brain wave patterns, the formation of new neuronal pathways and the reconfiguration of brain tissue. This makes it even *more* efficient at what it does – and what it does is to listen to orders! The brain physically rewires itself in order to optimise the regular thinking patterns based on what the brain is 'commanded' to do. Our thoughts can *literally* change our brain and our body.

A fear-based 'selection process' is what many of us are programmed to adopt from a young age. The threat to our survival, acceptance and fulfilment is consistently emphasised by the media, our education authorities, the government, multi million dollar industries who profit from us thinking in this way and sometimes even those who care about us - like our well wishing parents, friends and relatives. The inability to discern creates *imbalance* on an individual and on a global scale. Our survival instincts are constantly sensitised through these avenues and as a result we have become efficient at 'boxing ourselves in' to an emotional *safe zone*. Staying in this confined place, we go against our natural desire to grow and expand *with* the Universe. This discord, this contraction, creates energetic dis-ease within us, which presents itself as emotional, physical, mental and spiritual problems. It is my belief that this discord is the *major* root cause of virtually all of the suffering we see in the world.

Although we may not have complete control over our external environments, we do have control over our internal environment.

The mastery of *this* environment leads to inevitable change in the external and creates a ripple effect that impacts the entire energetic field that we are all an integral part of. This not only positively impacts our lives but it also helps to balance the *Yin* and *Yang* energies – the contracting and expanding energies of the planet.

The key to mastering our thoughts, our internal environment and our lives is to recognise that **we are not our thoughts**, that they are comparable to *possessions* we have accumulated and attached ourselves to over time. The mere fact that we have the ability to sit back, close our eyes and consciously *watch* the contents of our minds and our thoughts in action, suggests that there is *another* aspect of ourselves that is observing. It points to a deeper layer of ourselves being in operation. Being in this energetically *detached* state allows us to analyse and question the validity of our thinking habits and direct them for our own benefit.

You are the awareness beneath thought, which means that your thoughts can not define you. Just like a body part can not define who you are, a thought, a belief or a conviction can not either. They are very much separate, superficial and external to your real *core* self. Success comes from understanding this principle and from detaching from our thoughts enough to see them in operation. Awareness is the *primary* step in the sifting, sorting and selection of beneficial thought, to channel towards our desires. Detachment from our thoughts allows us to see with *clarity* and to consciously select the direction of our mind. When we attach who we are to our thoughts and *identify* with them i.e. make them responsible for our identity, we are directed *by* them. When we detach from our thoughts, we are back in the driver's seat of our lives. We harness authentic power by creating *space* between our observing mind and our thinking mind. By refining this art, you are no longer a victim and you become a conscious creator of your destiny. The ability to observe thought is a form of meditation - a heightened state of awareness. This process helps to take us back to our core self and puts us back in charge of our physical realities. This form of personal power is authentic, magnetic and *influential* and has its foundation firmly built on positive *internal* influence.

Chapter 3: We have two voices

An old Cherokee is teaching his grandson about life.

*"A fight is going on inside me," he said to the boy.
"It is a terrible fight and it is between two wolves. One is evil —
he is anger, envy, sorrow, regret, greed, arrogance, self-pity, guilt,
resentment, inferiority, lies, false pride, superiority, and ego."*

*He continued, "The other is good — he is joy, peace, love, hope,
serenity, humility, kindness, benevolence, empathy, generosity,
truth, compassion, and faith. The same fight is going on inside
you — and inside every other person, too."*

*The grandson thought about it for a minute and then asked his
grandfather, "Which wolf will win?"*

The old Cherokee simply replied, "The one you feed."

We all have two 'wolves' — or the two *voices*. How we nurture the
different voices has the *greatest* impact on our lives, our well being,
our emotional states, our relationships, our success levels and (at
the most quantum level) the electromagnetic field generated by
the body - often referred to as the *aura*. The aura strongly reflects
our emotional states and extends beyond the physical body,

creating impact on our surroundings. When our emotional state and energetic output is of *high* vibration i.e. when we feel the most loving or when we are feeling the happiest, our aura can expand out to fill an entire room.

'High' and 'low' vibration are terms used to describe the characteristics of energy. Energy travels in waves between 2 extremes: shortest in wavelength and fast (HIGH vibration) or longest in wavelength and slow (LOW vibration). The lower the vibration, the denser the energy is. A table is made up of atoms connected by energy vibrating at a much *lower* vibration than water, for instance, which has a much higher overall vibration making it lighter and more fluid than the denser table. Meat has denser energy than fruit, making fruit a 'higher vibrational' food. The spectrum of our emotions are also of varying vibrational frequency. Being in love emits energy of higher vibration than being depressed - which emits a lower, denser vibration. The differing emotional states that we are in have a significant impact on the quality of our physical states, our auras and our surroundings. The higher our vibration, the more energy we feel and the greater our capacity to influence our environments. The quality of our aura becomes more energetically *cohesive* (or organised) when in loving, excited states making us extremely powerful, magnetic and charismatic.

Our energy field is connected to and *overlays* the background field that makes life possible. It is a well known fact of quantum science that the slightest movement creates an energetic impact on the *entire* web. Our energetic influence, in the form of thought, emotion and action, can be compared to the *tugging* of one of the corners of this infinitely large blanket – movement or bending of one aspect, impacts the whole. Effectively when we move, even at the most atomic level, we affect the field at every possible point. Our emotions and our actions have a strong influence on the field and therefore our lives – this may seem obvious. What may not be obvious is that we are all connected at the most profound, elemental level, to each other and to the 'web' of life. We interact with *everything* around us, all of the time, whether we realise it or not. The higher our vibration, the greater the fluidity of our energy and the greater its influence on the web of life and everything to do with it.

As a result of this deep connection, we have the ability to influence and can, in turn, *be* influenced by each other and our environments. Any energetic change within you, including your thoughts, will impact the *entire* cosmos at the most elemental level and any energetic change in the cosmos will impact *you* at the most cellular level. The importance of this *'field'* has been emphasised by virtually every culture from around the world - from modern day and going back thousands of years – with references to it and its geometry in and around ancient carvings, diagrams and text. Due to our influence on this field, we are incredibly powerful. Every thought creates a *measurable* electromagnetic wave that is perceivable on subtle levels by others and our environments. The mind is the *powerhouse* and the most crucial, underlying determinant of our influence and of our growth. It is, therefore, of extreme value to recognise and understand the major players – the two voices - that exist within it.

So what are these forces - the two voices?

One of these voices is often referred to as the **Ego**. The Ego is *loud*, manages and assesses risk, takes on board and logically organises past information, forms our identity based on experience and has an innate tendency to *fear*, constantly looking out for risks to our survival and for methods of preservation. It places great significance on our 'accumulations' - including our thoughts, beliefs, ideas and possessions, which the Ego relies upon to form our identity. The Ego can be extremely useful in *life threatening* situations where plenty of information and 'tried and tested' safety measures are warranted but in those who have an overactive, 'hypersensitised' Ego, symptoms related to chronic fear can develop due to the Ego's *hyper-vigilance* in these states. We use the term 'egotistical' often. An egotistical person displays *false* confidence and an unhealthy attachment to some 'thing' - whether it be a thought, belief, possession or identity, in order to compensate for a lack of self worth. In the traditional sense, an 'egotistical person' displays symptoms of *fear* − the fear of not being accepted or being worthy without some form of 'accumulation'. An overactive Ego mind, however, is not limited to this definition only and can relate to *any* expression of fear, such as aggression, worry, anxiety and frustration. In this sense, fear − which stems from the Ego mind − expresses itself in multiple different ways despite being commonly associated with a form of arrogance.

The Ego seeks to keep us safe and out of danger. Its foundation lies in historic experience and it perceives *all* painful events as 'dangerous' in nature, including emotionally painful events. These events can involve those we have directly experienced or even those which we have learned of. Anything with a negative emotional attachment can become a reason for the Ego to operate. In any given situation that is considered by the Ego to be a potential threat to survival, it will draw out information from the past - a whole host of thoughts, memories, justifications and experiences - in order to analyse the risk and prevent the undertaking of a particular 'harmful' action. A mental 'case' is prepared. This process may not necessarily be instigated by a physical threat (for which the Ego mind is best suited) but can also bleed into perceived emotional threats, such as the threat of disconnection from others or a lack of acceptance – both of which are basic human needs. Due to its bolshie nature, the Ego demands to make its concerns known and can be the loudest, most dominant voice in our heads. In genuinely dangerous situations, the Ego is perfectly suited and of huge benefit to us but when the threat is not necessarily life threatening, the Ego often has a 'Bull in a China shop' approach.

Effectively, when we think fear based thoughts, the Ego is in play. The Ego mind is a highly evolved, 2-million-year old *tool* that is concerned, solely, with survival of itself and you, as its 'carrier'. As with everything *other* than the observational mind, the Ego mind is very much a separate entity to our core selves. Any event that validates its need to be in operation will enhance its existence and the more validation it gets, the stronger and more influential it becomes. Like all forms of energy, it can build tremendous momentum. It is one of the strongest forces that is in operation on the planet and unless balanced through awareness, it has the ability to steer our lives towards feeling chronic fear based emotion.

The Ego is extremely intelligent, efficient and powerful. When it is not operating in harmony with our entire being - suffering exists. When we look around us we may recognise ways in which an imbalanced and a hypersensitive Ego can be *validated* by its surroundings. This can stem from advertisements for cosmetic products - which can feed the fear of not being accepted in an authentic form, to the threat of inadequacy in the presence of someone who is more affluent or feelings of insignificance and subsequent aggression during an altercation. Often the Ego, with its assumptions based on fear, attempts to make *any* external situation a potential threat to survival and therefore demands we pay regular attention to it and them! Not only is this draining and mentally distracting, it is quite often completely unnecessary.

Sustained fear based emotions stemming from the Ego have the general property of *contracting* our energy and causing weakness - mentally, physically and energetically - leading to the subsequent stagnation of our growth. Fundamentally, the Ego wants to protect us from danger and can become our ally if we learn to manage it. We need to place it, with the respect it deserves, from the drivers into the passenger seat of our lives. Self mastery depends on our ability to sift through unconscious, programmed thinking patterns in order to eliminate those thoughts that are not *real* threats to our existence but are in active operation. Personal power surfaces when we use the powerful Ego, rather than it using *us*.

It is human nature to avoid pain and seek pleasure but the *associations* we make with each can either help us to grow and *empower* us or limit and *disempower* us. These associations are wired into us based on the consistent thoughts (*beliefs*) that we think. Being able to detach from these thoughts *enough* to see them clearly, helps us to create mental associations for *positive* benefit and growth and to clear the ones that do not. For instance, if you are looking to get fitter and take up exercise, rather than attaching pain to the physical activity of exercise, you can learn to attach pain to the *lack* of it. By associating pleasure *with* physical exercise and associating pain with its *absence* and by reinforcing these associations, we can use our minds to help us grow and expand towards that which we desire. For this to happen, we must increase our awareness so we may understand what it is that we attach pain and pleasure *to* and how our current/past experiences have influenced this process. We need to differentiate between pain that encourages growth, pain that leads to limitation and genuine danger. We can be masters of our lives by learning to discern, by learning to see 'clearly' and by becoming more conscious of our internal make up.

The second voice is the voice of the **Heart**. It is the quiet, non imposing *'magician'* that speaks to us via visceral feeling opposed to mental thought. The Hearts' voice offers us encouragement and profound wisdom. In order to 'hear' it, we must cultivate *deep* listening skills i.e. listening with *every* part of our physical being. For this reason, it is important that we are connected and increase our sensitivity to changes that occur within the body. We need to learn to travel outside of the thinking mind and expand our awareness to incorporate our entire being. This is readily observed in young children and animals who live moment to moment, being guided by their feelings and emotions opposed to their logical thought processes.

The voice of the Heart lives predominantly in the present moment. It is the opposing 'love based' energy of the Ego – the opposite end of the same 'stick'. When a fear based thought is in operation the opposing Heart based feeling is always accessible.

Understanding this can help us to move from Ego based thought to Heart based feeling – moving us out of lower vibrational, disempowering states and into higher vibrational, empowering ones. Learning to listen to the Hearts' voice allows us to build energetic momentum on Heart based feeling, which guide us to our joys and passions. **The *merging* of the Ego voice with Heart centred wisdom is the aim.** This enables us to move towards our passions in a way that avoids *actual* harm.

The Hearts' voice does not fear and offers encouragement, courage and self esteem - contrary to the wary Ego. When nurtured and balanced against the Ego, the voice of the Heart is our greatest friend. It is humble in its approach and does not demand attention like the Ego does. Instead it patiently waits for you to tune into it. By moving from Ego to Heart, from thinking to feeling, from a negative to a positive mind set, we raise our energetic vibration enough to tune into *higher* vibrational forms of intelligence, such as intuition, creativity, genius inspiration and universal knowledge.

It only takes for us to study the innate intelligence of the body to gain some idea of the intelligence that these higher forms of energy have. This intelligence is responsible for the creation of *all* of nature. When we tune in to this intelligence, it predominantly communicates *via* the Heart, leading to an undeniable knowingness and urge to act. This urge can be supported by the Hearts' encouraging 'words' when the Ego is tamed. By paving the way for heart centred, higher intelligence to emerge, we connect with a flawless form of loving guidance. This is often why, throughout time, we have been encouraged to 'follow our hearts'. This intelligence guides us towards our deep seated desires – if we deliberately choose which 'voice' to nurture.

There is a tendency to want to see the Ego mind as the 'enemy' and often people who try to align with their purpose will attack this aspect of their being. We forget that the Ego is there for an important purpose and therefore warrants respect and appreciation. It appreciates loving kindness. Unknowingly, we tend to give the Ego mind further justification and permission to thrive, as we feed it *more* fear in the form of our *own* fear of its presence. Understanding the Egos' role in justified situations and recognising its value allows for the complete acceptance of that aspect of *ourselves*. Accepting it is true wholeness, acceptance of who you are and a form of unconditional love directed at yourself. This is the foundation of *all* forms of unconditional love. Resisting the Ego acts to empower it into further imbalance. Once we appreciate it and accept it for what it is, the Ego mind takes a 'back seat' and operates as a peaceful, useful ally and emerges in the presence of *actual* danger. It does not feel the need to demand attention consistently.

The merging of the Ego with Heart centred wisdom and the harmonious combination of the two innate energies, act to cultivate a powerfully expansive and extremely intelligent driving force. The key to moving towards our passions is to not attach and to *unidentify* with *any* of the thoughts and feelings that occur within us and from that place, to select and follow through on those feelings that are Heart centred opposed to Ego based. The Ego can thereafter be utilised to carry out the practical steps. The fusion between Yin and Yang, light and dark, Ego and Soul is true wholeness, unconditional love and integrity. It provides the fertile soil in which our unique gifts can grow and creates space for higher minded attunement. This is the balance to strive for in order to propel ourselves into expansion and to experience the deep fulfilment that comes with it. And it all comes from the expanded awareness of who we are.

Chapter 4: What is Consciousness?

In spiritual terms – *Consciousness is our ability to SEE.*

To define the term 'seeing' is not as simple as it may seem. For instance, when asked to picture a red car, which aspect of you is it that sees the car in that instant? It is surely not our physical eyes which see what is physically present. In this case, we use a *deeper* vision. The same principle applies if you were asked to visualise something that has never been seen with the physical eyes before – such as a green, luminous, elephant or even your dream life. In this sense, *seeing* in the traditional sense isn't necessarily the true, *complete* definition of vision. It points to alternative forms of vision being available and in operation, a branch of which is imagination. It also points towards the difficulty in defining the term 'seeing' and what it is that 'sees'.

Here I am sitting on a chair typing these words. Looking at the chair, I see it has four legs, a seat, two arms, a cushion and a back rest but if I could see the chair as atoms through a microscope, as elemental, I would see it as vibrating, charged particles held together via energetic bonds and the whole structure of the chair would be predominantly empty space. When we look at the night sky, many of the stars that we can see do not even exist any longer. What we see is light travelling to our eyes well after the death of the star. Immediately the definition of 'seeing' and *what* we are seeing is subject to debate. This highlights the limitation of seeing with our physical eyes and the differing degrees of vision. None of the perspectives are correct or incorrect, good or bad ways of seeing - merely varying degrees of vision from altered levels of consciousness.

"As above, so below"

– Hermes Trismegistus

Every living being, including plants, insects, animals and ourselves, operate from varying degrees of *pure* vision or consciousness, quite like being able to see the chair in the above example from alternate viewpoints. Pure consciousness can be compared to the *broadest* perspective and seeing at the most elemental level – at the *purest* form of reality. Below this level of vision, life operates at varying degrees of consciousness. As a result of the various 'forms' that are perceivable, it may be clear to see that everything exists on *multiple* levels, from physical form through to energetic form. All of these forms exist and they do so simultaneously. This points to expanded and multiple versions of *ourselves* operating in existence too. Pure vision, or pure consciousness, is seeing form at the most energetic level - far beyond what modern science allows at this stage of our evolution. Pure consciousness is the highest, most expanded viewpoint - seeing at the level of the energetic blueprint. So the purer and more expanded our consciousness, the closer we are to the background, foundational 'field' of energy that makes life possible and the broader our perspective.

Pure consciousness and the background field of energy are the same, in essence. It is that aspect of life that *'thought'* the Universe into manifestation; the energy that gave birth to all aspects of life. Just as *'some-thing'* can not be formed from *'no-thing'*, the Universe can not be formed from a complete lack of existence. It exists as a result of a greater level of consciousness – one that is of pure potential – a Divine 'spark'. Call it the Big Bang, call it Pure Consciousness, call it a thought – the principle is the same. Furthermore, the process that thought the Universe into reality is the exact same process *we* adopt when we put thought into action. In essence, the more creative potential we have, the greater our level of consciousness and vice versa. Our thoughts are the pure potential that lead to creation on a personal level and it is thought, stemming from a *higher* mind, that leads to creation on a Universal level. The difference in our creative potential lies in our ability to 'see' based on how conscious we are and therefore our ability to connect with the *field*.

Where a lioness may operate solely from the level of consciousness that drives her to hunt, we may be able to operate from *this* level of consciousness as well as from the level that makes us feel compassion for the prey. These are just two differing levels of consciousness – one is a broader perspective than the other. As we learn to see from broader or higher perspectives, we 'ascend' up the ladder of consciousness. Technically, it is less of an ascension and more of an expansion into our broader, elemental form. There are *infinite* levels of consciousness and therefore infinite forms that are in operation.

51

So long as the Universe continues to expand exponentially, this will always be the case.

'Everything you can imagine is real'

- *Pablo Picasso*

The ability we have to become aware, grow and alter our levels of consciousness is what makes us powerful as human beings. Our ability to raise our personal vibration (through the deliberate choosing of thoughts that lead to more *loving* emotional states) and the subsequent ability to have broader minded perspective is linked to our success on all levels. This *limitless* potential for the growth of our consciousness is what helps us to see and THINK our versions of reality into existence – whether they be desirable or not. The nurturing of our emotions and our consciousness is what leads to the creation of desirable circumstances in our lives. This is a *core* principle adopted by some of the most successful people on the planet. Those that are able to create and fulfil their desires have understood the significance of emotional mastery, creative visualisation, broader minded perspective and have attached energetic fuel to the process through building momentum on high quality thought. Knowingly or unknowingly, these are the steps underpinning EVERY creative process based on a vision stemming from broader minded perspective. The broader the perspective, or the more expanded our levels of consciousness, the greater the vision and our capacity to influence our realities.

In spiritual terms, being conscious is more than just the ability to have differing perspectives or viewpoints. It is a deep *connection* to the field of pure potentiality and the 'tuning in' to its properties. This connection to the field, or *Source* energy, cultivates an innate knowingness and awareness of reality, or 'truth', at the most fundamental level. It also allows us to *draw* upon the energy of the field and its creative, inspirational essence.

The reason why we as souls pass from lifetime to lifetime is in an attempt to evolve and reach this heightened state of pure consciousness; to reconnect with our Source and to remember who we are. It is not a reaching in fact, it is more of a 'stripping back' to get to our core essence. The Souls energy, like any form of energy, can never be destroyed – it only changes form. Depending on the vibration of our energy, we will have the ability to expand rapidly or slowly. We can be compared to a crystallised ice cube, which has a dense vibration. Source energy can be compared to steam – the most fluid, expanded state to be in. Aspects of Source *crystallise* into form, including those aspects that contain our 'accumulated' vibrations across lifetimes, giving us our physical, unique human existence. We 'bring down' our varying vibrational states. *Unlike* the ice cube, however, we can alter our vibrational states by the deliberate adjustment of our thoughts and emotions. Our energy is made 'denser' through negative emotion, which always stem from fear and can be made 'lighter' through positive emotion. Denser personal vibration hinders our growth, literally 'weighing' us down energetically.

Positive, loving emotion *raises* our vibration, placing us in and connecting us to expanded states.

Our experiences mirror our emotional states – the closer we are to vibrating at the same level as Source, the greater our ability to expand, to create and make positive influence in our lives. Pure consciousness is referred to as 'truth' as it is the purest form of seeing. It is a crystal clear form of clarity of 'all that is', not only from the deepest quantum level but also from the highest, most 'birds eye' perspective. Pure consciousness encompasses *all* perspectives and all forms. When our limited consciousness merges with that which is infinite consciousness, it is referred to as *Enlightenment* – a state of seeing with pure clarity, a state of pure creativity and seeing the perfection of the *whole*.

It is only ever in the *absence* of clarity that we feel powerless, confused and disempowered. The greater our levels of consciousness (and therefore clarity), the more empowered we feel. It is difficult to feel stressed, depressed or anxious about things that you have *maximum* clarity over, therefore the expansion of personal consciousness is of paramount importance to our wellbeing.

Understanding that we have limits on our consciousness helps to keep our minds open to the possibility of *more* and allows room for growth. Unless we expand our consciousness beyond our limited perspectives, thoughts and beliefs and release our attachments to them, it is impossible to see the Divine, perfect order of all that occurs within our lives. Without seeing this, we feel powerless, uninspired, stagnant and hopeless. When we connect to something greater than ourselves, our *Higher Self*, life is full of possibility.

The reason why the varying degrees of consciousness exist in the first place, is two fold:

The first reason is for **EXPANSION**. Source energy is responsible for the creation of the entire Universe and all forms of life. It is the underlying layer of energy holding all form together. In order for the Universe to expand, which it does so constantly and exponentially, we have *separated* from this energetic 'pool' of pure consciousness and this separation exists in varying degrees. The separation is responsible for fear and the lack of power that we may feel, depending on the degree of separation. The most extreme end of the separation is often termed the 'Alpha' and pure consciousness is often termed the 'Omega'. They are both different facets, the opposing energies of the whole.

This may lead to the question - *how does separation lead to expansion?* It may even sound somewhat cruel. In order to answer this, picture the use of a bow and an arrow. In order for the arrow to propel forwards, it needs to be pulled back i.e. there needs to be separation. The further back the arrow on the bow is pulled back, the further forwards it will go. This analogy points to infinite cycles of creation. Everything that expands is balanced against an equal and opposite force going in the opposite direction. Spiritually speaking, this is the role of difficult times and feelings of disconnection in our evolution. The purpose was never to stay in a 'retracted' position, but to use periods of disconnection (and their associated fear based symptoms) to move forward with greater intensity and to expand. Those who are considered to be *offensive* in their actions or who appear to create 'problems' in the world are actually playing their role of separation at an extreme level… and dare I say it − for the greater good!

The difficulty is that staying in a separated state is encouraged in many ways. Society, mass media, our upbringing, pain and suffering and generally many external factors 'keep' us in this separated state whilst we are unaware of them. As well as this, many energetic forces play a role in encouraging separation which, from a broader perspective, are actually for the greater benefit of personal and collective expansion. To those who are 'unconscious', these aspects of life encourage them to stay *stuck* in a separated state. This was not the intention behind the initial separation. We have been equipped with the Ego mind to help us to navigate safely back to our powerful selves. It serves to avoid danger and should be used as a tool but we have misinterpreted the function of the Ego mind as mentioned previously. Many of us have learnt to live in sustained states of fear. This chronic state of separation may bleed into how we feel about ourselves, others and the world and affect our ability to love and appreciate innate uniqueness in ourselves and in others. It prevents our growth.

The second purpose of the varying degrees of consciousness is for Source energy to **EXPERIENCE** itself.

'We are not a human being having a spiritual experience, we are spiritual beings having a human experience'

- Pierre Teilhard de Chardin

You are an *aspect* of infinite consciousness focussed into a particular point in space and time and as such, you represent a *unique* aspect of this pure consciousness. This makes you *Divine*, *perfect* and *powerful*. Like pure Source energy, you also have creative abilities that stem from thought, in the same way that the Universe was created by it – through pure potential. But why, you may ask, does pure consciousness/Source energy need to do this? What is the purpose of this type of experience? How does it experience itself in this way? The reason is very simple and I will explain using the example of eating an apple. No matter how much you read, think, imagine or educate yourself on an apple, the taste of it can not be compared to the *experience* of eating it. In the same way, Source energy experiences itself *through* your existence and your creations. The fact that you are alive, have form and the ability to *think* is a testament to your greatness and proof of your innate connection. Pure consciousness has *thought* you into existence with the intention of experiencing a unique aspect of itself. When you see yourself as anything less than Divine and deserving of appreciation; any less perfect than you are, you do yourself and the creator a huge disservice.

'You are not a drop in the ocean, you are the entire ocean in a drop'

- Rumi

As mentioned in the previous chapter, the only reason why we may feel like this, the only reason why we would struggle to love ourselves in this way is due to an imbalance in our Ego mind which serves to protect us from feeling trauma. It learns very quickly, within the first 5-6 years of life, to trust the words, opinions and teachings of others in order to prevent the pain of further separation. We learn to act in a way that avoids the feelings of rejection. It is in our initial separation from Source energy that the Ego was formed. The more disconnected from Source we feel, the greater our Ego and our fears are in operation. Just as darkness is an *absence* of light, fear is an absence of cosmic, Source energy and the lack of connection to it. These symptoms present themselves as a whole host of negative, energetically *contracting* emotions, which affect our well being and quality of life. Effectively, the more disconnected we are, the less energy we have and the more disempowered we feel. These are symptoms of a breakdown in our primary relationship – the one we have with our higher being - Source energy.

The beauty of being in this human form is that we, inherently, have the ability to be on ALL scales of the spectrum of consciousness through choice and practice. Picture a hall of mirrors – we can be in any mirror through the adjustment of our vision. *We* are the Alpha and *we* are the Omega and we have the ability to choose the varying notes of love and fear that reside in between. In order to expand your level of consciousness requires nothing more than the regular observation of your current state and the deliberate change in your physical vibration through emotional mastery. It very much involves practice in residing in your deepest observational layer so that you may observe and consciously change your thoughts and emotional states. This connects you to infinite consciousness – a platform from which broader perspective, perfect vision and clarity is readily available. All it takes is for us to feel good and the growth takes care of itself.

Chapter 5: Intuition – the third voice

Intuition quite literally means '*Inner Teacher*'. When the five sensory feedback system, historic memory, Ego voice and the interpretation of our external environments is silenced; when the mind is stilled, *space* is created for higher forms of communication. We 'tune in' to the background consciousness, in which we all reside and which resides in everything - the field of pure potentiality. It is the underlying 'thinking' and creative aspect of the Universe. By raising our vibration and travelling into deeper states of our being, we return to our core essence and cohere with the high vibration of Source energy. This energetic cohesion closes the gap between the *Alpha* and the *Omega* freeing us from symptoms associated with separation. The feelings that we experience as a result of our disconnection from Source (and therefore our *higher* selves) leads to energetic 'misalignment' and fear. By changing our states from fear to love helps us to reconnect back to our Source. In fact, how we feel is a direct reflection of the strength of our connection.

Intuition is the energy created within us that is *independent* of pre-existing thought and feeling – it has no dialogue and no rational basis. It is a *surge* in pure creative energy and a form of direct communication from Source that occurs in the absence of energetic resistance. Intuition is a strong, independent 'gut feeling' that is not based on conscious reasoning. It is an innate knowingness and a compulsion to act which is linked to the pre-frontal cortex of the brain. The intuitive communication from our expanded selves does not occur by means of language or vision. This is because language is limited due to its potential for multiple interpretations and physical vision is also limited, as mentioned in the previous chapters. The way we interpret *all* external stimuli is subject to limitation. For this reason, intuition and higher forms of intelligence do not communicate with us in these ways. Instead they communicate via *internal* physiological methods that are not subject to doubt or misinterpretation. They communicate by means of strong, undeniable visceral feeling, instinct, inner vision and emotion.

As mentioned previously, whenever we stray from our connection to Source, our higher being, our primary relationship, we immediately feel a sense of separation and therefore the feelings associated with it - such as fear, anxiety, helplessness, a lack of control, depression, anger and sadness. When we align with Source, we feel positive feelings of connection - such as love, excitement, positive anticipation, creativity, inspiration, healing and joy. This is how the 'in – built' emotional guidance operates within us. It is designed to *assist* us in our alignment with Source which enables our personal expansion and expression. When we align with Source, all expansive thoughts, feelings and desires, even those that are not in our conscious awareness, are supercharged and the creative process begins.

Expansion, as the term suggests, is a natural, *resistance free*, form of being. Source energy brings about expansion by means of our connection to it. Our higher vibrational states allow this connection to undertake and increases the overall energy in our body – almost like opening up an electric circuit to allow the current to pass through. This 'current' floods our energy body and the energy of our deep seated desires - all we have to do is allow it to flow by consciously removing 'resistance' in the form of denser, negative energy. Whenever we take steps to raise our vibration and feel *good*, we reap the benefits of our connection to Source. The *'how will it happen?'* questions are looked after and we are guided to take the relevant steps towards our expansion via our intuitive communication. Source energy is intelligent, nurturing and encouraging and sustained connection leads to the development of authentic power. It has the broadest perspective of all, a perspective that we do not have access to. It can therefore be trusted to guide.

Anything that is considered 'powerful' suggests the absence of resistance and the same applies to our energetic state. In fact, it takes much force and *drains* energy to go against expansion and feel disconnected. Resistance is caused by contraction and contraction is caused by negative emotion. It presents as lethargy, lack of inspiration and external exertion of control – an inauthentic form of power. These symptoms are very much a consequence of not going with the 'flow' of the Universe or going *against* our connection to Source.

Regardless of external circumstance, we have control over our internal environments. We have the ability to access our authentic power and higher, broader perspective just by raising our personal vibration. Just by changing one thought to another, we have the ability to connect with our expanded self, to see the bigger picture and remove limits on our perspective. Just as all forms of nature have the ability to thrive in supportive environments – expansion and growth are innate potentials that we are born with. We are *born* to be successful by nature. These states 'thrive' when the resistance is melted. So it is not so much about achieving success through *external* effort, it is more about removing the barriers that are in the way. The only thing that restricts that growth is our own limited, accumulated thoughts and the subsequent energetic contraction that arises from them. Energetic expansion or contraction is solely based on our ability to choose thoughts that encourage one or the other. Whilst we are in an 'unconscious' state and whilst we are unaware of the thoughts that circulate in our minds, our minds will carry out the selection process automatically – in 'auto pilot'.

When we maintain our connection, space is created for intuitive guidance. Our receptivity and awareness become heightened and we are offered *all* of the gifts of Source energy - pure creativity, inspiration, passion, wisdom, problem solving abilities and broader perspective. This intuitive communication is enhanced by Heart centred wisdom which works in harmony with the Intuition. All that is required is the clearing of resistance which presents as lower vibrational, Ego based thoughts and paving the way for connection. This is brought about by becoming aware of the Egos' influence.

'The intuitive, metaphoric mind is a gift and the rational mind is a faithful servant'

- Albert Einstein

Recognising intuitive guidance requires practice and a heightened state of awareness. It is necessary to 'de-program' ourselves from unconscious, repetitive cycles of thinking and to learn how to be mentally present. This creates space and allows us to be able to *detect* guidance. We have to learn how to become sensitive to *feeling* changes within our bodies. Connection with Source energy is heavily dependent upon the observation and understanding of our minds and bodies in their *natural*, resistance free states. This is a state we experience when we are young children. By learning how to get back to a similar place energetically – a place free of energetic 'density' – we recognise intuitive guidance more readily. By shining the light of consciousness onto our fears and insecurities we clear the path for higher intelligence. Without awareness of our resistance free states, we have no baseline to measure intuitive feeling against. Furthermore, if our minds are not in the present moment, we are far too mentally busy to notice.

One of the best ways to tap into your intuition is to learn how to still the mind, to ask a question and feel a response in the body. An expanded feeling in the body relates to confirmation. Contraction is disapproval from your higher mind. The other methods of communication can be inner knowing, visualisation and hearing. Bear in mind that as intuition has *no rational basis* and therefore the responses can not stem from the mind or any pre-existing thoughts that occur in there. The feelings are very much located in the body and are spontaneous. They occur separate to the mind and its logical thinking patterns.

Intuitive guidance becomes harder to sense as we transition through life being taught how to think, feel and act, which effectively *numbs* us and reduces our sensitivity to fluctuations that occur within the body. We get accustomed to operating in a mechanical way, constantly thinking and being 'in our heads'. Unless we have the ability to increase our sensitivity to detect these fluctuations, we miss regular signals, signs, feelings and communication from Source and our higher expanded beings. This sensitivity increases through simple awareness, mindfulness practices and learning to be mentally present.

Throughout life, rational thinking processes are prioritised over those that focus on feeling and sensitivity. This form of programming is responsible for the disconnection that we feel on a personal and on interpersonal levels. It is also responsible for the limitation in our Divine connection and potential. The chronic neglect of our emotions and feelings has created widespread imbalance. The importance placed on the *head* over the *heart* presents itself as worldwide suffering on subtle and grand scales. In fact, the majority of the suffering we experience in the world is a result of this imbalance and our deteriorating connection with infinite consciousness. We are suffering from symptoms of disconnection.

The good news is that we can strip back the layers and *unlearn* what we have learnt. The power of mental presence paired with increased sensitivity to intuitive guidance is a natural state of being and a gift we can nurture. Moving away from being in the future and past tenses mentally and moving from head to heart allows us to connect with our *greatest* source of energy. This is our primary relationship – the one that we have with ourselves.

Chapter 6: Finding your Purpose

If it doesn't excite you, it's not the right path

Our purpose *surfaces* in the presence of passion and passion is revealed in the absence of fear. Where there is *pure* passion (and its counterparts - the vibration of genuine *gratitude* and *appreciation*) there is no room for fear – there is no space for the two opposing types of energy to exist together. It defies quantum law. When we feel *genuinely* grateful for something, fear is dispelled and space is created for excitement and passion to emerge. It is virtually impossible to feel any kind of negative emotion when feeling genuine gratitude. Our true purpose starts to reveal itself as our conditioned fears are recognised and cleared. *This process occurs in direct proportion.* Our purpose in life is very personal and is linked to a **core challenge** in our lives. Our work lies in bringing awareness to the multiple influences of fear in our lives, including our core fears and working through them to find our purpose i.e. what we can teach the world about our transition from fear to empowerment. It is in the sustained commitment to the process of understanding ourselves, understanding what makes us 'tick' and processing fear based beliefs that we align with that which brings us the greatest joy, excitement and passion. It is in the *inward* journey that the outward journey is reflected and revealed.

Energetically we draw upon that which mimics our emotional states from the *ether* – the invisible unrefined, raw form of energy that our senses are generally unable to detect but which is present all around. The quality of our emotional states and their subsequent attraction can be seen in our environments and circumstances. Just as steam can turn into water and water into ice, our emotional states are the *catalysts* that draw upon the etheric 'steam' which, with sustained focus, crystallise into 'ice' or physical form. We create in the *same way* that we are created. When we attach a thought to its corresponding emotion it builds momentum and impacts the etheric field. If this is sustained, the energy will build until the desired outcome is achieved. If, however, we *think* that we want more wealth but our emotions are focussed on how it feels to *not* have it i.e. you feel scarcity emotionally, momentum will build toward our emotional state *regardless* of what we think. Our emotions will impact the etheric field, due to their stronger energetic influence and you will attract even more scarcity. Like emotions attracts like circumstances.

This process of attraction can occur rapidly or very slowly (even spanning over multiple lifetimes) dependent upon our mental focus, emotional intensity and the momentum that has built. This may sound simple enough - it makes sense that if we put our minds to a task, it can come about – but the emphasis here is on the energy of our emotions which are quite often underestimated. To create on a small scale, the clarity of our thoughts, the intensity of our emotions and the overall refinement is not so critical. To create on a large scale however (i.e. to change our lives for the better) our thoughts need to be more refined, our emotions need to be more streamlined and the actions (which is the easy part) actually take care of themselves. Action becomes natural and full of enthusiasm – it just *flows*. Emotional integrity and emotional energy is vital when it comes to the creative process yet many fall into the trap of acting without taking the steps to align their thoughts and emotions first. Without taking these steps, 'fractures' can appear in our energetic projection and therefore our manifestations - and the creative process can lose its sense of fun! This makes logical *and* energetic sense.

Emotions have a major influence on our energy. The more positive and loving our emotions (which includes love directed at *ourselves*) the greater the *quality* of the energy that is projected by our body. There is increased cohesion in our energy field i.e. it becomes more organised, stronger and more expansive. The more expansive our energy, the more influence it has on our surroundings. At our highest emotional states, our ability to connect with the highest energy of *all* increases as we mimic its state. This higher state of energy is the background, foundational, deepest possible 'canvas' of life - Source energy. Being an expanded aspect of ourselves, Source energy acts alongside our emotional desires, acting upon the ether to bring about our desires at a Soul level.

Energy can not be destroyed, it only changes form and the energy of our Soul becomes 'imprinted' by the energy of our desires and our fears. These imprints of our emotional states onto our Soul, manifest themselves in our lives at some stage or another. We can direct *what* is manifested by bringing ourselves, our emotions, our fears, our desires and our *entire being* into awareness - from which place, we can select which vibrations to act upon and which to consciously 'clear'.

The process of manifestation not only applies to our active conscious thoughts and their attached emotions but also to our subconscious thoughts, which have the potential to go completely unnoticed. Whilst in an unconscious state, we may unknowingly allow these thoughts to run in the background, like a software program, whilst they build momentum and intensity. These background vibrations have the potential to attract unfavourable circumstances over time if they are 'low vibration' in nature. The only way we can direct our lives towards favourable circumstances is by becoming more aware of which thoughts are in operation and getting to know ourselves on deeper levels, so that we may become *conscious* directors of our lives.

Our circumstances and external environments act to show ourselves **to** ourselves, not as a means of punishment or reward but by means of Universal law. This is the premise of *karma* – you get back what you give out. Just as warm climates attract birds in winter by use of the electromagnetic grid of the earth - we also create an electromagnetic *pull* on the ether of the Universe via the projection of our thoughts and emotions. In this example, we are the warmer environment, the birds represent our circumstances and our energetic state creates the magnetic 'pull'. As it stands in this example, we will attract to ourselves circumstances that *harmonise* with our environment i.e. those that mirror our state.

Every undesirable experience in our lives offers us the opportunity to reflect on those aspects of ourselves that require attention or readjustment. Picture life to be a constantly running movie and our subconscious/conscious thoughts, as well as our Soul imprints, being the *projectors* creating the scenes. These scenes are dictated by the quality and the nature of the energy we project. Life is the most realistic hologram of our perceptions which can be used to assess the projection of our energy – but it is a hologram nonetheless. As mentioned previously, there is virtually no substance to any structure. What we see around us is a beautiful dance between energy and light – and not much else. The projector of our minds *bends* the light to create the reality around us. When we clear our limited, lower vibrational, ingrained perceptions, a form of healing takes place – the 'lens' of the 'projector' becomes clearer and we 'shine our light'. We start to become *whole* and this starts to reflect in our lives.

'Thoughts are Universally, not individually, rooted'

- *Paramhansa Yogananda*

Being part of the expanded consciousness, or the underlying *fabric* of energy, everything that we ever aspire to achieve, or think about, is present all around us in raw, **unrefined** forms of energy - regardless of their perceptibility. Every 'thing' and every raw 'ingredient' exists around us, in *processed*, physical form and *unrefined*, energetic form. *All* form that we see around us is the manipulation of energy at a quantum level. If we can imagine something, it already exists in energetic form otherwise it would be impossible to perceive – the energetic *configuration* of that thought form has to come from somewhere before it is sensed and brought into our awareness. It is not spontaneously created in the mind – energy can not be created or destroyed.

If you were to fill up a pantry with every single ingredient known to man, you could imagine the most unique recipe using the ingredients and it would be possible to achieve. The pantry can be compared to the Universe that contains all of the ingredients and the pantry door, the point of creation. Some 'recipes' may be more difficult to create than others and may also require more refinement, some may not even be a success, but effectively, if you can imagine it, it is possible to find the ingredients to construct it from this abundant, Universal pantry. The same stands true for the manifestation of our desires. Even a *thought* has been drawn down from the ether, where infinite thoughts and their corresponding energies exists.

The Universe is where every single Universal 'ingredient' is available. This includes what is tangible and what is not – including the energetic configuration of our thoughts, as mentioned above. Everything *beyond* our observational mind is a tangible, external form of energy – a raw ingredient. Our thoughts have substance. The Universe is an infinitely abundant place where our imaginative potential and therefore, our creative potential, is endless. This has been the fundamental understanding of *every* great inventor, creator and manifestor that has existed throughout time.

Although it may be the norm for us now, there was a time when the idea of a 500 tonne, aluminium alloy flying through the skies was completely absurd but now the reality of the common airplane is a perfectly accepted aspect of our lives. The creation of the plane came about in the same way – the gradual building of layers of energy through focus and vision, based on quantum law, until its physical formation.

Effectively, everything we could possibly think of, want or even imagine is all around us in etheric form and in order to fulfil our desires, we can use Universal laws to process them into physical form. Like in the pantry example, the raw ingredients are available to us but it is in the studying, careful selection, measuring and *alignment* of ingredients followed by the 'cooking' process that we create. Similarly, the fulfilment of our desires is driven by vision (the recipe), the selective choosing of our thoughts (the ingredients), balancing our emotions (measuring of ingredients) and bringing all component parts together. It is a *flawless* recipe. Passion or love create the perfect 'cooking' environments due to their high vibrational and energetic influence on the ether. Fear, effectively, turns the 'oven' *off*.

Our *true* purpose and the fulfilment of our desires is not exactly the same thing -albeit intertwined. Desire can be based on a foundation of fear whereas true purpose is a complete absence of it. For instance, we may desire the accumulation of money based on the positive association between money and increased opportunity and the ability to be *more* of who we are. If we desire money based on all the positive emotions associated with it, if we can emotionally *feel* its presence to bring about an energetic change, our desire can be fulfilled – this is passion and happens in the absence of fear. On the flip side, the desire for money can also develop due to an associated fear and being in a place where there is a *lack* of it. A constant feeling of not having enough money and its associated fear can lead to a desire by *default* – a desire to break free from fear, perpetuated further by fear. This emotional state is not driven by love and therefore does not direct us toward passion. Our purpose comes together when we *merge* our passions.

Passion is *independent* of our circumstances and fear based emotions. Our purpose is the bringing together of our passions – like the pieces of the jigsaw puzzle coming together. Our purpose reveals itself when the energy of Source (the highest vibration) meets the energy of our personality at *its* highest vibration.

Desire based on fear and desire based on unconditional love (passion) is often quite difficult to differentiate because:

Fear can *disguise* itself as Love.

Love has the potential to be mistaken for the absence of *discomfort.* This is a limiting, incomplete form of love which is not the pure, authentic love that is necessary for growth or for revealing our purpose to us. Pure love is boundless and unconditional, and is not determined by the presence or absence of any external factors.

If, for example, you develop a fear of travel, as a result of being told as a child that the world is a dangerous place to be in, you may grow up being less adventurous and less inclined to explore your surroundings. You may perceive this as a 'love' of being indoors or a 'love' of safe routine. It is, however, love by default. It is influenced by a preconceived belief system about the world in general, based on a foundation of fear. So as comfortable, as safe, as warm and as *fuzzy* as it may feel to stay indoors all day, to someone who has this belief system, these feelings of 'love' are actually fear in disguise.

In a similar way, we may be lulled into a false sense of love throughout our lives, based upon limiting beliefs about ourselves and others. We may be in romantic relationships that are unloving, because we have a fear of being alone, or we may stay in unfulfilling jobs for years because we believe that we are unable to do better. We may confuse love with 'playing it safe' and put a ceiling on our fulfilment, which is effectively a lack of love for ourselves.

Fear is comfortable. Love requires courage.

Following on from the above point, where it may be clear to see that 'playing it safe' emotionally may not be a true indicator of authentic love, we move on to another difference between love and fear in an attempt to answer the question – *how do we know the difference between the Love and Fear in order to find our purpose?*
There is no growth without discomfort. Love encourages growth and fear is restrictive. Love requires the courage to push through discomfort and fear restricts us to a comfort zone. A comfort zone feels very safe but in order to expand and grow through experience - which I believe is the purpose of life - discomfort and pain shouldn't be *'avoided at all cost'*. They are the true indicators of growth and should almost be embraced. Having the courage to face and move **through** adversity, to *allow* personal growth, is the ultimate act of self love - and self love is the foundation of

ALL forms of unconditional love. So, remember, just because it is comfortable, it doesn't necessarily mean you are on the path of love – and if you are not on the path of love, you are on the path of fear instead.

Fear is programmed into us. Love requires self discovery.

In order to be on the path of love, we go against thousands of years of conditioned thinking patterns. That means that sometimes it is easier, and almost *encouraged*, to give in to fear. Throughout generations, whether it be deliberate or not, we have been taught to be fearful of a whole host of things, from actual danger to beliefs about how we look or dress and even how we should and should not think. By being programmed to *think* and *feel* in a particular way, we lose the ability to do either - and authentic love does not disable us or others. Love requires emotional intelligence and self awareness which is not readily taught by modern society. This fear/love imbalance in our *internal* environment is responsible for a whole host of emotional and mental imbalances that we see in society today. Fear, insecurity and a lack of self worth become advantageous, not just monetarily to large institutions but even to *ourselves*, as we become convinced that we are benefitting by thinking in a fearful way – we can get lulled us into a false sense of security. Whenever we think thoughts such as '*I can't do it, so I won't try*' or '*I'm not good enough*', we are suffering from symptoms of this imbalance - an imbalance that we were not born with but one that we have learnt.

So how do we break the cycles of fear based thinking? By becoming more *conscious* of our own fears, by bringing our 'darkness' into the 'light', by merging the *Yin* and the *Yang* aspects, by knowing ourselves and by becoming aware of how we think. We break the cycles of fear by choosing the course of our thoughts and our lives – the path of Love or the path of Fear. Through self awareness and connection to our bodies, we can free ourselves from the bondage of fear, live a peaceful, loving and joyful life and become a source of inspiration for others.

Love is power. Fear is force.

Being in a loving state should empower and excite you. It should make you feel energetic since love *expands* energy. Fear backs you into a corner and restricts you with force. Love is therefore powerfully expansive and activates passion. In any given situation, choosing love, in the absence of fear, on a strong foundation of self love, directs you towards your passions and your fulfilment. Being in this sustained state will always guide you towards recognising your purpose. This form of thinking aligns you with your natural state of being, your true essence and tunes you into a powerful source of loving/expansive energy that guides and directs you towards your Souls purpose.

'Opportunity is missed by most people because it is dressed in overalls and looks like work'

\- *Thomas A. Edison*

When we have discovered our purpose, when we are aware of what we want, when we discover those ideas that get us out of bed in the morning with joyous enthusiasm, the next step is to **ground** our passions into physical form. This is the second phase of manifestation – the external aspects. Just thinking and emotions alone (the internal aspects) will not bring about enough momentum for physical reality to manifest itself. The great thing about grounding, is that it's the easiest part. When the thought and the emotion are aligned, physical creation happens with ease due to the amount of energy that is behind it. It becomes more difficult, in fact, to take *no* action. We have done this our entire lives, yet in order to have the life we desire, we need to become conscious creators rather than unconscious ones so that we may direct our lives towards our passions rather than towards our fears.

Creation occurs at three levels – **the thought, the word and the deed**. Our thoughts need to be aligned with our words AND our words need to be aligned with our actions. In order to manifest successfully (whether it be consciously for our growth or unconsciously for our contraction), all three need to operate in harmony and with integrity – they must mirror each other.

For example:
You want to make a cup of tea.
First comes the awareness that you are thirsty, then comes the internal
dialogue and thought resulting in 'I will have a cup of tea', then comes the act
of making the tea.

In the above example, from the awareness of thirst comes the
thought. From the thought comes the *word* or the internal dialogue
and then comes the *deed* or the action of making yourself a drink.
Awareness and action are relatively automatic but the thought
and internal dialogue is where the greatest influence lies. It is
mastering at this level that we create maximum impact on our
lives.

The recognition of subconscious and conscious thinking patterns
assist in the awareness of our inner, mental make up from which
place thoughts and circumstances that benefit us can be *consciously*
selected and emphasised and those that do not can be *consciously*
given less focus. The *emphasised* thoughts then become our
emotional, and therefore energetic state - the vibrations of which
we emit into the Universe and ultimately attract back to us
electromagnetically. The idea is to allow ALL thoughts the entry
into our mind space, not to control any of them. From the
wonderful array of thought options and external circumstances
available, we can choose our mental direction based on the those
that make us feel the greatest levels of love and excitement i.e. we
can operate from a higher vibrational state. Aligning our
thoughts, with our words and our deeds 'clears the path' for
Universal energies to infiltrate our being, acting as a source of

inspiration, guidance, support and a driving force behind the fulfilment of our desires.

'If you are depressed you are living in the past.
If you are anxious you are living in the future.
If you are at peace you are living in the present.'

-   Lao Tsu

Thoughts stemming from the past and based on the future are hugely influential in our fear based thinking – a habit of thinking that we have all developed in our lives at some point or another. When we use our minds to access the the past and future tenses as and when required, rather than residing there, we learn about the huge benefits of presence. The present moment is where we can feel wellness and peace; where our minds are still and where we have greatest influence. It is also the place where we are able to 'listen' to inner and Universal wisdom. Presence is where we can move *out* of our busy minds and connect with our bodies, which prompt us to our vibrational states and put us back in touch with our personal power.

Finding our purpose is a process that can take days, years, decades and even lifetimes. This process, however, can be accelerated through a number of practices to 'weed' out fear and raise our awareness – techniques that are from both modern day and going back *thousands* of years. They are tools that raise our vibration and support the will and commitment to understand ourselves and clear subconscious, restrictive thinking patterns. Such tools include contemplation, meditation, mindfulness, breathing techniques, energy healing, yoga, chi kung, floatation, sound vibration, binaural beats and many more. These practices are based on bringing ourselves back to our centre, bringing our minds back to the present moment, connecting with ourselves on deeper levels and tuning in to our true power.

Chapter 7: What is Alignment?

Energetic alignment is a fusion between defragmented aspects of our being. It exists at two levels:

1. At the ***physical*** level: the alignment of what we think, what we say and what we do.
2. At the ***non - physical*** level: the alignment of our conscious mind, our subconscious mind and the superconscious mind.

Wholeness comes from the merging of the physical with the non-physical. Alignment is the single greatest catalyst for wellbeing, abundance, connection, peace of mind, overall success and fulfilment of desire. When aligned, we connect *deeply* with our inner being, our broader minded perspective and Source energy. We become *powerhouses* for change.

PHYSICAL alignment.

Physical alignment occurs when what we *think*, what we *say* and what we *do* are in harmony. When these three factors are out of alignment, fragmentation of our energy occurs. This leads to the creation of a somewhat 'disconnected' vibration which is emitted from our body into our auras and into the ether, impacting all three energetically. This discorded energy is 'sent out' which, with enough momentum, attracts experiences of a similar nature - whether it be discord within our bodies or discord in our circumstances.

For instance, if you are in the pursuit of accumulating money, your actions may be aligned with this desire and so may your words but if you *think* that money is difficult to obtain or if you associate money with difficult emotional experience, your resultant energetic vibration will be fragmented. Similarly, if you are in the pursuit of love, you may have underlying beliefs about love that are limiting based on painful historic experience. Unless your sense of awareness is raised enough to be able to observe and clear these limiting beliefs, your actions, words and thoughts will work against each other to create energetic resistance – or defragmentation.

We are, innately, extremely powerful creators. We constantly create the circumstances and experiences around us. The only factor that prevents us from creating *desirable* circumstances for ourselves, is the amount of energetic resistance we build throughout our lives. What this suggests is that *all* the good things in life are ready to flow to us since we are connected to the background, abundant, flawlessly creative, energy field. This connection gives us life and boundless opportunity but it is in the lack of this connection that we prevent our creative abilities from mirroring that of the energy that creates worlds!

The process of creation occurs at the level of thought. What we *say* (internal and external dialogue) and what we *do* are the resultant symptoms of the momentum that is gained by our thoughts. The alignment of all three is a powerful force that leads to the manifestation of desires. It is therefore important for us to become regularly aware of our thoughts in order to *fuel* the manifestation of our desirable outcomes. Our emotions and their associated physical responses, are of extreme value when it comes to recognising which thoughts are in operation. By themselves, thoughts can be difficult to identify but with the help of our bodies, we can understand our mental make up with greater ease. For example, thoughts which relate to grief can cause contraction in the chest and thoughts associated with shame can cause contraction in the pelvic area of the body. As mentioned previously, for us to recognise the regular signals that our bodies are giving to us, we must increase our sensitivity to the minor and major changes that occur within them. This sensitivity allows us to recognise deviations *away* from resistance-free, centred states.

Alignment can not occur without 'unearthing' resistant conscious and subconscious thoughts and their associated feelings. This is because without their awareness, even if they are not present in the conscious mind, they can impact our physical vibration. The good news is that since our external environments i.e. our thoughts, our emotions, our physical states and our circumstances are reflections of our internal states, life is consistently reflecting our vibration back to us. The trick is to be able to identify these 'lessons' and to use them as platforms to grow. The *awareness* of resistant thoughts is a form of energetic 'clearing'. The process becomes more efficient over time with practice in increasing our sensitivity levels and in regularly residing in the present moment and in our observer mind. Some of the vibratory 'imprints' can also come from past lives since the nature of energy is that it can not be destroyed and can only change form. These imprints on the Souls energy can either encourage expansion or contraction i.e. they can be based on love or based or fear. They can be transported into and be in operation in our current lives. All of the resistant energy of our being becomes easier to identify as we go 'up' the sensitivity scale.

NON PHYSICAL alignment.

This level of alignment occurs when the *subconscious, conscious* and *superconscious* minds operate in harmony with each other. These are the three levels of consciousness that are in operation at any given time.

The conscious mind is the platform we operate from during our daily activities and during waking hours. It represents only a small portion of our consciousness and is the aspect of our mental processing that we can think and talk about in a rational way. It is the logical aspect of our minds. The conscious mind involves all of the things that you are currently aware of and thinking about. Things that the conscious mind wants to keep hidden from our awareness, such as painful memories, are repressed into the *subconscious* mind where they do not necessarily have a strong logical basis. These subconscious thoughts can be drawn upon through conscious awareness and via various methods and 'triggers'. The conscious mind is somewhat akin to short-term memory and is limited in terms of capacity.

The subconscious mind accounts for approximately 80% of our consciousness and lies *below* the level of conscious awareness. Its physical seat in the body is in the lower brain and the spine. It records *everything* that we do or have done, including every activity we have ever engaged in, our thoughts about those activities and their associated emotions. For the most part, this aspect of our consciousness remains hidden from our everyday awareness and often 'leaks' into our conscious minds in disguised form. An example of this is when historic memory is triggered by even a *loosely* linked external event, leading to an extremely realistic and influential mental *overlay* on our present circumstance.

The subconscious mind has tremendous influence on how we think and act when in a conscious state. Those influences are from past actions and the subsequent habits that we have formed from them. What this means is that ideas that are drawn from the subconscious mind are not *new* or *creative* in nature and operating from this aspect of our minds is limiting and repetitive. When the subconscious mind is understood and cleared of denser energies and thoughts, it provides a channel for the communication between the conscious and the superconscious mind.

The superconscious mind encompasses a level of awareness that sees both material reality and also the *energy* behind that reality. Through observation, clearing and the raising of our personal vibration, we melt resistance which allows us to *tune in* to superconsciousness. Superconsciousness is also known as Source energy, God, the Universe or the Field. The superconscious is where *true* creativity is found and as a result of our connection to it, we draw upon the creative potential that has created all that is. Expressions of this kind of creativity are distinctive from those that come from the conscious or the subconscious mind – they are new, innovative and represent expansion. Truly great works of art, music, the greatest scientific discoveries and the deepest spiritual experiences are found in the superconscious mind.

"We have to remember that what we observe is not nature herself, but nature exposed to our method of questioning"

– Werner Heisenberg – founder of Quantum Mechanics

When we raise our energetic vibration and consciousness to access the superconscious mind, we have the ability to access the thoughts that are available on *that* level of consciousness. These thoughts are universally available to those who tune in at this level. Similarly, if we live mainly on conscious or subconscious levels, we operate using thoughts from those respective levels. Due to its nature, operating from a purely conscious mind we see *distinction* between us and others but operating from a superconscious level we are less limited in our perspectives and are able to see the underlying unity – the energetic reality – behind outer form.

The merging and unity of all of the aspects of our being – our thoughts, feelings, emotions, dialogue, actions, sub, super and conscious minds is heavily dependent on and directly related to the *awareness* of all aspects. With awareness comes spontaneous clearing.

Alignment opens us up to higher forms of intelligence, true creativity, a deep sense of wisdom, inner knowing and pure vision. We see the perfection of all of life. We shift from the smaller, personality mind to our expanded, Divine, *higher* mind and are able to live out our authentic essence.

Chapter 8: Fill up your cup

Alignment and our connection to Source energy is heavily dependent on the *state* that we operate in. Our physical state is a reflection of our emotional state. The more *empowered* our state, the higher the vibration of our energetic output and the more connected we feel.

A powerful, healthy, 'high vibrational' state occurs in the presence of good feeling emotion, such as happiness, joy, exuberance, love and hope. This state is reflected in our physical bodies too and we feel more energetic and motivated. A 'lower vibrational' state leads to feelings such as depression, sadness, loneliness, anger, despair, anxiety and hopelessness. This, too, is reflected in our bodies as an overall *reduction* in energy. Effectively, lower vibrational, fear-based emotions create an internal state that enhances resistance and prevents growth. It also prevents cosmic, Source energy from flowing into our energy body which in turn affects our alignment with it.

Our physical and emotional states are a reflection of our thoughts. The conscious, deliberate selection of 'good feeling' thoughts has a direct impact on our emotions and our body. Similarly, changes in our body have a direct impact on our thoughts and emotions. They are all interlinked. Understanding our state, at any given time, by becoming aware of our thoughts, emotions and how our body feels can put us in a place of control, where we can alter our vibrational output. Initially it is much easier to gain information on the quality of our states by connecting with and detecting changes in our bodies, as the momentum of energy is the greater than our thoughts at this level. Over time and with practice, as our sensitivity increases, we are able to detect changes in our mental balance i.e. at the point of creation.

All you have to do is take the first step

On a strong foundation of self love, self care and attention, we are able to *love* ourselves into higher states. By becoming aware of that which brings us discomfort, *honouring* our emotions enough to pay them attention and by soothing the associated thoughts into thoughts of a loving nature, we change the frequency at which we vibrate. At times this may involve removing yourself physically from a situation that causes vibrational imbalance at other times it may involve choosing thoughts that feel better – being the 'calm in the storm'. Emotions such as gratitude and appreciation are powerful states to be in, strong enough to create a state in which lower vibrational thoughts, stemming from fear, can not exist. As mentioned previously, it is almost impossible to feel negative emotion when we feel *genuine* gratitude. Training our brains to reside in these states is of huge value when it comes to creating desirable outcomes. Starting the day with feelings of gratitude, creates energetic momentum in the direction of our desires – it leads to expansion of our state and strengthened connection.

By commencing the process of manifestation i.e. finding and selecting a single positive aspect to focus on that feels good, energetic momentum starts to build. Thoughts of a similar nature get drawn upon to create further momentum. Your energy body expands and you vibrate 'higher'. Over time, alignment takes place and you connect with the all encompassing field. From this place, *more* energy is drawn from the expanded, abundant Source which aligns *with* you. It presents to you circumstances, situations and people that help you to close the gap between you and your Souls purpose. Following the Heart centred wisdom by means of your intuition, you can use *feeling* to move into *action* which creates further expansion and desirable circumstances – representative of an even greater level of energy, momentum and connection. This is a journey from head to heart - an energetically flawless, *tried and tested* formula. All you have to do is take the first step.

Protecting your energy.

As your energetic sensitivity increases, it is not only possible to tune in to changes that occur within *your* personal energy field, it is also possible that you will tune into the energy fields of others. Just as important it is to be able to discern higher vibrational thoughts from lower vibrational ones within ourselves, it is equally as important to discern which energies exist within you that are *yours* and which energies belong to others. Some people can walk into a room and light the entire room up, others can drag the vibration down. Often we can take on the energies of those around us, adopting them as our own. As a result, we can create momentum based on *their* energies. It is vital to protect your energy and your energetic 'vessel' from lower vibrational energies in order to continue your expansion. Bear in mind that if this 'protection' occurs as a result of fear, this can go against the purpose of alignment! Unconditional love is the goal as it is the *highest* frequency that we can resonate at. This level of unconditional love must spread to *ourselves* in order for us to be whole and for us to operate from a place of vibrational integrity. Practising *energetic* detachment from our thoughts and from others and by operating from a place of deep observation creates space for unconditional love to blossom. The result is that we *emit* loving energy rather than absorbing denser energy. This is not only an act of unconditional love aimed at ourselves but also directed at others. Energetic detachment moves us away from dependency and is the path towards higher forms of love – an act of loving service at the most *fundamental* level.

Being in an 'observer' state and detaching from our thoughts and emotions to be able to see them, takes time and practice. The first stage is to acknowledge changes in our states and to *accept* them for what they are. The second stage is to observe them from a distance. Sometimes the extent of detachment needs to be greater i.e. physically removing yourself from a situation and at other times it requires nothing more than mentally creating 'space' by changing our minds. Which ever method is adopted is it important to understand that there is no 'right' or 'wrong' way.

Our evolution towards unconditional love and the detachment from our thoughts occurs in the presence of increasing our understanding and the awareness of who we are. It is for this reason that the greatest philosophers and teachers of our time have placed massive emphasis on **knowing yourself**. This simple yet profound statement encompasses the entire contents of this book. It summarises the key to our success in two simple words, the explanation of which has been the aim for this piece of writing.

I hope that this aim has been achieved. If nothing else, I hope this book has opened your mind to some degree and inspired you to carry on your search for greatness. *Seek and ye shall find.* Dare to have vision, it costs nothing. My wish is that fear never holds you back. What you desire is attainable. If you can imagine it, the energy of it already exists in the ether. Understand and train your mind. A successful mind-set attracts success in life. Feel free to test out the simple concepts in this book – it is my assurance to you that, like me, you will never look back.

To end on the words of Dr. Wayne W. Dyer:

'While the world of reality has its limits, the world of your imagination is without boundaries. Learn to recognise the signs of habitual ways of being and then learn to shift your thinking to being in balance with your dreams'

Chapter 9: Future Events

Join myself and my 'Soul Family' at our '**Get Conscious**' camps - where you can learn how to connect with your Body, Mind, Intuition and your Higher Minded perspective.

Visit
www.GetConscious.co.uk
for more details

Follow us on Facebook and Instagram at *'Get Conscious'*

Email us for individual and corporate bookings at:
info@getconscious.co.uk

'Until you make the unconscious conscious,
it will direct your life and you will call it
fate.'

- Carl Jung